MW00961953

JONAH
THE RUNAWAY PREACHER

The Story of Jonah
accurately retold from the Bible by
CARINE MACKENZIE

Design and illustrations
Duncan McLaren

Published by
CHRISTIAN FOCUS PUBLICATIONS
Houston, Texas, USA   Tain, Ross-shire, Scotland

© 1989 Christian Focus Publications ISBN 0906731 66 6

Reprinted 1992

Jonah was a Hebrew man who lived in the land of Israel. He loved the Lord God.

One day God spoke to him, giving him a very important message. 'Go to the great city of Nineveh. Tell the people there that I see their wicked-ness.'

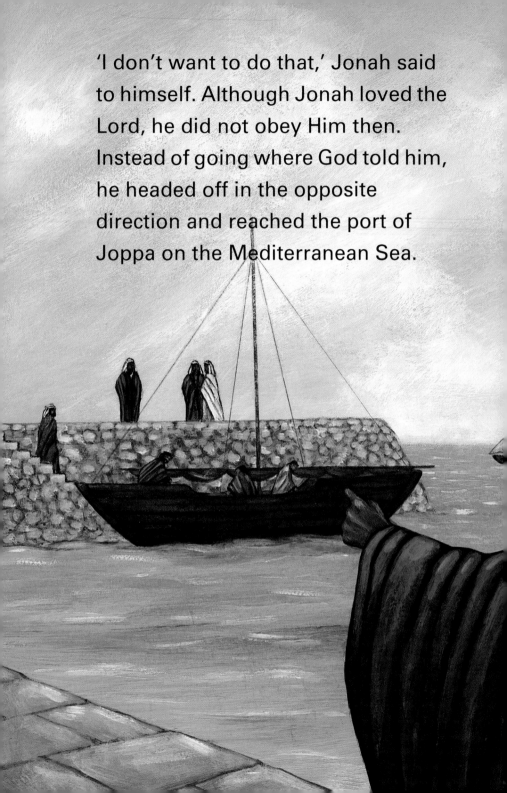

'I don't want to do that,' Jonah said to himself. Although Jonah loved the Lord, he did not obey Him then. Instead of going where God told him, he headed off in the opposite direction and reached the port of Joppa on the Mediterranean Sea.

God gives us commands in His Word, the Bible. Very often we are like Jonah and do what we want ourselves instead of what God wants us to do. This disobedience is displeasing to God.

At Joppa, Jonah found a boat ready to sail across the sea to Tarshish.

Jonah paid the fare and boarded the ship. The ship set sail, with Jonah down below as one of the passengers. He thought he was escaping from God and the difficult duties that God was placing on him.

Jonah was soon to learn that no one can run away from God.

God was seeing Jonah in the ship too. God is seeing us wherever we are. He sees us at home, at school, in the street. He still sees us when we are in a place where we ought not to be.

God, who is in charge of all weather conditions, sent a violent storm on the sea. The storm was so wild that it seemed that the ship would soon be broken up.

The sailors were scared. They threw the cargo overboard in order to make the boat lighter. That did no good. They were very worried. They prayed to their own false gods but of course they could not hear them. Only God, the Lord, can hear and answer prayer.

Through all the commotion, Jonah
was fast asleep down below in the
sides of the ship.

The captain came down and shook
him awake. 'What do you think you
are doing, sleepy head? Get up and
pray to your God. Perhaps He will
save us from perishing,' he said.

'Why has this disaster happened to
us?' one man asked. 'Who knows?'
answered another. 'Let's draw lots
and see who the blame will fall on.'

So they cast lots and it so happened that the lot fell on Jonah and so he got the blame. This was not decided by chance but by God directing the whole matter.

The other men immediately pounced on Jonah. 'You are to blame! Tell us why! What do you do? Where do you come from?' The questions flew from every side.

Jonah told them, 'I am a Hebrew. I worship the Lord, the God of Heaven who made the sea and the dry land. I am trying to run away from the presence of the Lord God,' he added.

The men were very afraid. 'Oh, why have you done this?' they moaned.

Even these heathen men realised that Jonah had done wrong, but the sea was getting rougher and rougher.

'What will we do to you, so that the sea would be made calm again?' they asked him.

Jonah's solution was very drastic. 'Take me and throw me overboard into the sea. The sea will then be calm. This is all my fault,' he said.

The men were reluctant to throw Jonah into the sea. They rowed as hard as they could in the direction of the land but with no success. No matter how hard they rowed they could make no headway and the sea grew even wilder than before.

These men, in desperation, cried in prayer to the Lord God. 'O Lord, please do not let us die because of this man Jonah. Do not blame us. You, O Lord, have done just what pleases You.'

With these words they caught Jonah and threw him into the raging sea. Down, down went Jonah into the deep.

The sailors on board the ship were astounded. The moment Jonah hit the water, the sea became calm.

These men saw the power of the true God. They saw His control over the wind and the sea. They worshipped God there and then on the deck of the ship.

We can see God's power every day in the world around us. This should make us worship and praise Him.

What had happened to Jonah? Was that the end of him? No. God still had work for him to do.

God made all animals and fishes and has them in His control. God had arranged that a great big whale would swallow Jonah.

For three days and three nights Jonah lived inside the whale. He had air to breathe and so was saved from drowning.

Jonah was in great trouble. He cried to God in prayer while he was in the stomach of the whale.

'I cried to God because of my trouble and He heard me. You have brought me into great trouble in the depths of the sea. When my soul was fainting, I remembered the Lord. I prayed to You. Salvation is of the Lord.'

Jonah worshipped God, confessed his wrong doing and thanked Him for His goodness in saving him.

God spoke to the whale and it vomited Jonah on to the dry land.

Jonah had another opportunity to obey God's voice. God spoke to him a second time. 'Go to the great city of Nineveh and preach to the people whatever I tell you.'

So Jonah went to Nineveh, a long way to the east. Nineveh was a huge place. Jonah entered the gates of the city and walked in towards the centre. He was here to preach the Word of the Lord. He had been reluctant to go at first but now he was not going to shirk his duty.

His message was loud and clear.
'In forty days time the city of Nineveh
shall be destroyed,' he proclaimed.

The people of Nineveh heard Jonah's words and they believed God. They were so sorry for their sins that they stopped eating food. They dressed in rough sackcloth. Even the King took off his beautiful robe and wore sackcloth like every one else. He did not sit on his throne. Instead he sat on the ground, in the ashes.

The King sent an order through the city. 'We must all cry to God. We must all turn from our evil ways,' he said. 'We must stop violence. Perhaps God will not destroy us after all.'

God took notice of the people of Nineveh. He heard their cries and He saw that they were truly sorry for their sins.

So God decided not to destroy the people of Nineveh.

Because of Jonah's message, many people were changed and served the true God. How pleased Jonah ought to have been. He had been used by God in converting many souls.

But Jonah was very angry. He was not at all pleased.

'This is just what I thought would happen,' he told God. 'I knew You were a gracious, merciful God. I knew You were very kind and would not destroy those people at all. That is why I decided to run away to Tarshish.'

Jonah was afraid that he would look foolish if his prophesies of destruction did not happen.

'Take my life away,' he said to God. 'It is better for me to die.'
'Do you think you are right to be so angry?' God asked him.

God then taught Jonah another lesson.

Jonah left the city in a bad mood. He climbed up on the east side of the town to a place where he would get a good view of all that was happening. He made a little shelter for himself and sat down to wait.

God, who has all plants in His control, made a creeping plant, with big leaves, to grow up. This gave very welcome shade to Jonah. He was very glad to sit under it in the heat of the day.

God has all the creeping animals in His control too. Next day God sent a worm to gnaw at the roots of the plant. The plant withered and died. No more cool shade for Jonah.

God, who is in charge of the winds, sent a very hot east wind. Jonah became hotter and hotter — so hot that he felt faint and very depressed. 'It would be better if I was dead,' he said to himself.

'Do you think you are right to be angry because the plant was destroyed?' God asked him.

'Of course I am right to be angry about that,' replied Jonah.

'You are sorry for that plant which you have not planted or tended. Should you not have as much pity for that great city of Nineveh as you have for a poor plant that grew in one night?' God replied.

Jonah himself had been wonderfully spared from destruction. He had been shown mercy. How he should have rejoiced that God showed mercy to thousands of people in Nineveh.

God's mercy is still being shown to sinners today. God's mercies are new every morning. We are told to 'Seek the Lord while He may be found, call upon Him while He is near. Let the wicked forsake his way and the unrighteous man his thoughts and let him return unto the Lord and He will have mercy upon him.'

The Lord Jesus speaks about Jonah. He compares Himself to Jonah. Jesus said that He would be three days and nights in the grave.

The Lord Jesus suffered this humiliation and suffering of death so that those who trust in Him would have everlasting life.